WORLD'S

FAVORITE

Easy To Play

ACCORDION

PIECES

FOREWORD

We are presenting a collection of about 100 of the most popular melodies of all time — arranged for the accordion. The emphasis in the musical arrangements is on simplicity without injury to the beauty or effectiveness of any of the compositions.

The selections will provide an interesting and entertaining repertoire of great variety, including popular music, spirituals, famous love songs, classics from the pens of the great masters, and simple tunes that everyone loves. They will guide the accordionist through his earlier studies into a higher degree of technical proficiency.

We offer this book in the hope that it will be very much enjoyed and treasured all through your musical career.

The Publisher

ASHLEY
PUBLICATIONS

DISTRIBUTED BY

HAL•LEONARD®
CORPORATION

7777 W. BLUEMOUND RD. P.O. BOX 13819 MILWAUKEE, WI 53213

CONTENTS

©Copyright 1960 by ASHLEY PUBLICATIONS, INC. •

International Copyright Secured   Made in U.S.A.   All Rights Reserved Including Public Performance for Profit

CLASSIFIED CONTENTS

THE STARS AND STRIPES FOREVER

March

JOHN PHILIP SOUSA

Marziale

Copyright © 1960—by ASHLEY PUBLICATIONS

International Copyright Secured.   Made in U.S.A.
All Rights Reserved Including Public Performance for Profit.

THE GLOW WORM

PAUL LINCKE

Copyright © 1960—by ASHLEY PUBLICATIONS

International Copyright Secured.   Made in U.S.A.
All Rights Reserved Including Public Performance for Profit.

WHEN THE SAINTS GO MARCHING IN

Copyright © 1960—by ASHLEY PUBLICATIONS

International Copyright Secured.   Made in U.S.A.
All Rights Reserved Including Public Performance for Profit.

VOLGA BOATMEN'S SONG

Copyright © 1960—by ASHLEY PUBLICATIONS

International Copyright Secured. Made in U.S.A.
All Rights Reserved Including Public Performance for Profit.

WILLIAM TELL
(Overture)

G. ROSSINI

Copyright © 1960—by ASHLEY PUBLICATIONS

International Copyright Secured.   Made in U.S.A.
All Rights Reserved Including Public Performance for Profit.

DANCE OF THE CANDY FAIRY

(Nutcracker Suite)

P. I. TSCHAIKOWSKY

Copyright © 1960—by ASHLEY PUBLICATIONS

International Copyright Secured.   Made in U.S.A.
All Rights Reserved Including Public Performance for Profit.

WASHINGTON POST MARCH

Marcato

J. P. SOUSA

Copyright © 1960—by ASHLEY PUBLICATIONS

International Copyright Secured.   Made in U.S.A.
All Rights Reserved Including Public Performance for Profit.

FIFTH NOCTURNE

J. LEY BACH

Copyright © 1960—by ASHLEY PUBLICATIONS

International Copyright Secured.   Made in U.S.A.
All Rights Reserved Including Public Performance for Profit.

EDELWEISS GLIDE

F. E. VANDERBECK

Copyright © 1960—by ASHLEY PUBLICATIONS

International Copyright Secured.   Made in U.S.A.
All Rights Reserved Including Public Performance for Profit.

BEAUTIFUL DREAMER

STEPHEN FOSTER

Copyright © 1960—by ASHLEY PUBLICATIONS

International Copyright Secured.   Made in U.S.A.
All Rights Reserved Including Public Performance for Profit.

DARK EYES

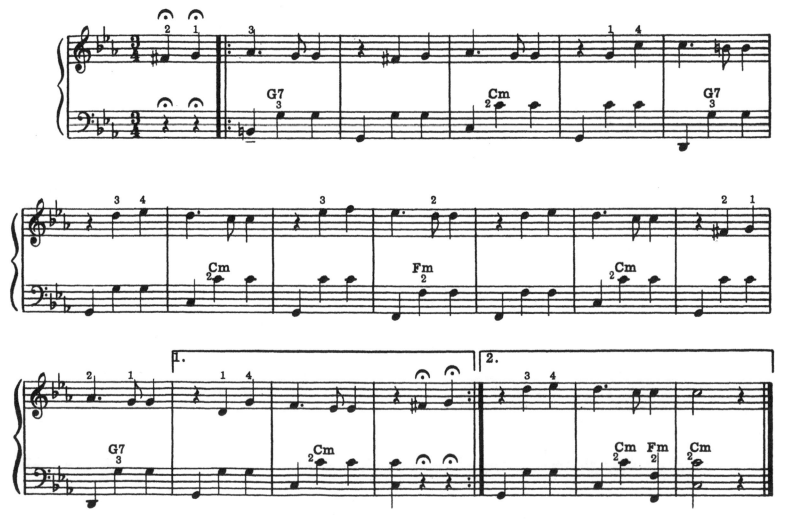

Copyright © 1960—by ASHLEY PUBLICATIONS

International Copyright Secured.   Made in U.S.A.
All Rights Reserved Including Public Performance for Profit.

CIRIBIRIBIN

A. PESTALOZZA

Copyright © 1960—by ASHLEY PUBLICATIONS

International Copyright Secured.   Made in U.S.A.
All Rights Reserved Including Public Performance for Profit.

BEAUTIFUL HEAVEN

(Cielito Lindo)

C. FERNANDEZ

Tempo di Valse

Copyright © 1960—by ASHLEY PUBLICATIONS

International Copyright Secured.   Made in U.S.A.
All Rights Reserved Including Public Performance for Profit.

BLACK HAWK WALTZ

M. E. WALSH

Valse moderato

Copyright © 1960—by ASHLEY PUBLICATIONS

International Copyright Secured.   Made in U.S.A.
All Rights Reserved Including Public Performance for Profit.

AVE MARIA

FRANZ SCHUBERT

Copyright © 1960—by ASHLEY PUBLICATIONS

International Copyright Secured.   Made in U.S.A.
All Rights Reserved Including Public Performance for Profit.

CONCERTO IN A MINOR

Allegro moderato con fuoco

E. GRIEG

Copyright © 1960—by ASHLEY PUBLICATIONS

International Copyright Secured.   Made in U.S.A.
All Rights Reserved Including Public Performance for Profit.

POEME

Tempo di Valse

Z. FIBICH

Copyright © 1960—by ASHLEY PUBLICATIONS

International Copyright Secured.   Made in U.S.A.
All Rights Reserved Including Public Performance for Profit.

NONE BUT THE LONELY HEART

P. I. TSCHAIKOWSKY

Andante

Copyright © 1960—by ASHLEY PUBLICATIONS

International Copyright Secured.   Made in U.S.A.
All Rights Reserved Including Public Performance for Profit.

MARCH SLAV

P. I. TSCHAIKOWSKY

Grave quasi marcia funebre

Copyright © 1960—by ASHLEY PUBLICATIONS

International Copyright Secured.   Made in U.S.A.
All Rights Reserved Including Public Performance for Profit.

TWO GUITARS

Copyright © 1960—by ASHLEY PUBLICATIONS

International Copyright Secured.   Made in U.S.A.
All Rights Reserved Including Public Performance for Profit.

MY HEART AT THY SWEET VOICE

C. SAINT-SAËNS

Moderato

Copyright © 1960—by ASHLEY PUBLICATIONS

International Copyright Secured.   Made in U.S.A.
All Rights Reserved Including Public Performance for Profit.

MEXICAN HAT DANCE

F. A. PATRICHALA

Copyright © 1960—by ASHLEY PUBLICATIONS

International Copyright Secured.   Made in U.S.A.
All Rights Reserved Including Public Performance for Profit.

D.C. al Fine

MEDITATION

J. MASSENET

Copyright © 1960—by ASHLEY PUBLICATIONS

International Copyright Secured.   Made in U.S.A.
All Rights Reserved Including Public Performance for Profit.

FANTASIE IMPROMPTU

F. CHOPIN

Copyright © 1960—by ASHLEY PUBLICATIONS

International Copyright Secured.   Made in U.S.A.
All Rights Reserved Including Public Performance for Profit.

FLOWER SONG

G. LANGE

Copyright © 1960—by ASHLEY PUBLICATIONS

International Copyright Secured.   Made in U.S.A.
All Rights Reserved Including Public Performance for Profit.

HABANERA

G. BIZET

Andantino

Copyright © 1960—by ASHLEY PUBLICATIONS

International Copyright Secured.   Made in U.S.A.
All Rights Reserved Including Public Performance for Profit.

51

LIEBESTRAUM

F. LISZT

Tempo di Valse

Copyright © 1960—by ASHLEY PUBLICATIONS

International Copyright Secured.   Made in U.S.A.
All Rights Reserved Including Public Performance for Profit.

LA DONNA È MOBILE

G. VERDI

Tempo di Valse

Copyright © 1960 — by ASHLEY PUBLICATIONS

International Copyright Secured.   Made in U.S.A.
All Rights Reserved Including Public Performance for Profit.

FÜR ELISE

L. VAN BEETHOVEN

Copyright © 1960—by ASHLEY PUBLICATIONS

International Copyright Secured.   Made in U.S.A.
All Rights Reserved Including Public Performance for Profit.

LA GOLONDRINA

N. SERRADELL

Tempo di Valse

Copyright © 1960—by ASHLEY PUBLICATIONS

International Copyright Secured.   Made in U.S.A.
All Rights Reserved Including Public Performance for Profit.

LA SPAGNOLA

V. DI CHIARA

Tempo di Valse

Copyright © 1960—by ASHLEY PUBLICATIONS

International Copyright Secured. Made in U.S.A.
All Rights Reserved Including Public Performance for Profit.

LA RASPA

Rather quick

Copyright © 1960—by ASHLEY PUBLICATIONS

International Copyright Secured.   Made in U.S.A.
All Rights Reserved Including Public Performance for Profit.

D.S. al Fine

LA CUMPARSITA

G. H. M. RODRIGUEZ

Tempo di Tango

Copyright © 1960—by ASHLEY PUBLICATIONS

International Copyright Secured.   Made in U.S.A.
All Rights Reserved Including Public Performance for Profit.

D.C. al Fine

TO A WILD ROSE

EDWARD MAC DOWELL

Copyright © 1960—by ASHLEY PUBLICATIONS

International Copyright Secured.   Made in U.S.A.
All Rights Reserved Including Public Performance for Profit.

SONGS MY MOTHER TAUGHT ME

ANTON DVORAK

Copyright © 1960 — by ASHLEY PUBLICATIONS

International Copyright Secured.   Made in U.S.A.
All Rights Reserved Including Public Performance for Profit.

SILVER THREADS AMONG THE GOLD

H. P. DANKS

Slowly

Copyright © 1960—by ASHLEY PUBLICATIONS

International Copyright Secured.   Made in U.S.A.
All Rights Reserved Including Public Performance for Profit.

be _____ al - ways young and fair to me. _____

SOUVENIR

FRANZ DRDLA

Copyright © 1960—by ASHLEY PUBLICATIONS

International Copyright Secured. Made in U.S.A.
All Rights Reserved Including Public Performance for Profit.

RAYMOND OVERTURE

AMBROISE THOMAS

Copyright © 1960—by ASHLEY PUBLICATIONS

International Copyright Secured.　　　　Made in U.S.A.
All Rights Reserved Including Public Performance for Profit.

SANTA LUCIA

Copyright © 1960—by ASHLEY PUBLICATIONS

International Copyright Secured.   Made in U.S.A.
All Rights Reserved Including Public Performance for Profit.

ROMANCE

Andante

JEAN SIBELIUS

Copyright © 1960—by ASHLEY PUBLICATIONS

International Copyright Secured.   Made in U.S.A.
All Rights Reserved Including Public Performance for Profit.

ROMANZE

R. SCHUMANN

Copyright © 1960—by ASHLEY PUBLICATIONS

International Copyright Secured.   Made in U.S.A.
All Rights Reserved Including Public Performance for Profit.

VIENNESE REFRAIN

Copyright © 1960 — by ASHLEY PUBLICATIONS

International Copyright Secured.   Made in U.S.A.
All Rights Reserved Including Public Performance for Profit.

POLONAISE

F. CHOPIN

Copyright © 1960—by ASHLEY PUBLICATIONS

International Copyright Secured.   Made in U.S.A.
All Rights Reserved Including Public Performance for Profit.

POLKA
(From "The Bartered Bride")

BEDRICH SMETANA

Allegro

Copyright © 1960 — by ASHLEY PUBLICATIONS

International Copyright Secured.   Made in U.S.A.
All Rights Reserved Including Public Performance for Profit.

SCARF DANCE

C. CHAMINADE

Copyright © 1960—by ASHLEY PUBLICATIONS

International Copyright Secured.   Made in U.S.A.
All Rights Reserved Including Public Performance for Profit.

ROUMANIAN RHAPSODY

GEORGES ENESCO

Copyright © 1960 — by ASHLEY PUBLICATIONS

International Copyright Secured.   Made in U.S.A.
All Rights Reserved Including Public Performance for Profit.

Più vivo

SABRE DANCE

A. KHACHATURIAN

Copyright © 1960—by ASHLEY PUBLICATIONS

International Copyright Secured.   Made in U.S.A.
All Rights Reserved Including Public Performance for Profit.

SCOTCH POEM

EDWARD MAC DOWELL

Copyright © 1960—by ASHLEY PUBLICATIONS

International Copyright Secured.   Made in U.S.A.
All Rights Reserved Including Public Performance for Profit.

SONG OF INDIA

NIKOLAS RIMSKY-KORSAKOFF

Copyright © 1960—by ASHLEY PUBLICATIONS

International Copyright Secured.   Made in U.S.A.
All Rights Reserved Including Public Performance for Profit.

WEDDING OF THE WINDS

JOHN T. HALL

Copyright © 1960 — by ASHLEY PUBLICATIONS

International Copyright Secured.   Made in U.S.A.
All Rights Reserved Including Public Performance for Profit.

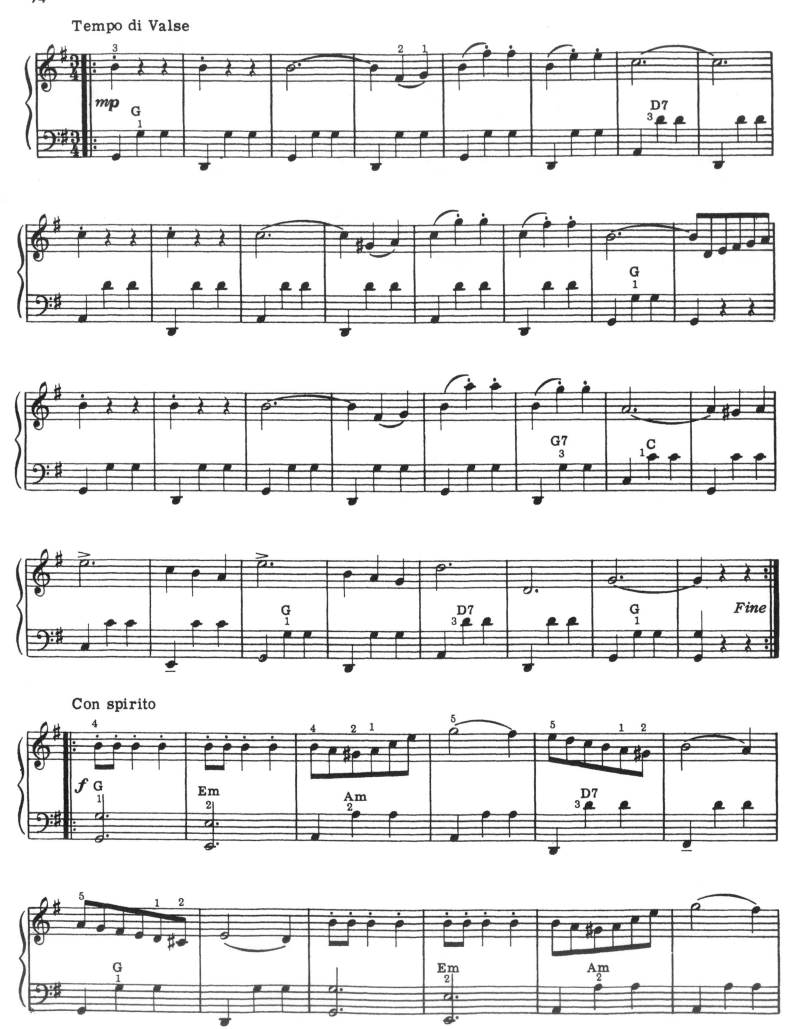

Con amore

LIGHT CAVALRY

F. VON SUPPE

Copyright © 1960—by ASHLEY PUBLICATIONS

International Copyright Secured.   Made in U.S.A.
All Rights Reserved Including Public Performance for Profit.

VIENI SUL MAR
(Oh Come To The Sea)

Tempo di Valse

See the moon cast its rays o'er the o-cean   Call-ing

lov-ers to sail o'er the sea   While my boat waits for

you when you wak-en   And to-geth-er how hap-py we'll be

But you lov-ers must wait while you slum-ber   As the hours keep

Copyright © 1960—by ASHLEY PUBLICATIONS

International Copyright Secured.   Made in U.S.A.
All Rights Reserved Including Public Performance for Profit.

RHAPSODIE HONGROISE No. 2

FRANZ LISZT

Copyright © 1960—by ASHLEY PUBLICATIONS

International Copyright Secured.   Made in U.S.A.
All Rights Reserved Including Public Performance for Profit.

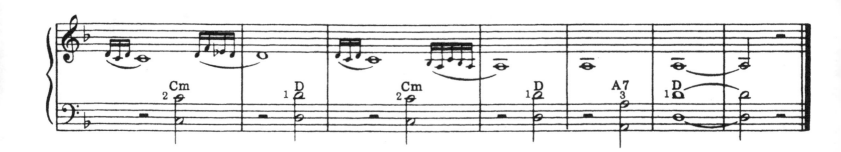

RUSTLE OF SPRING

CHRISTIAN SINDING

Copyright © 1960—by ASHLEY PUBLICATIONS

International Copyright Secured.   Made in U.S.A.
All Rights Reserved Including Public Performance for Profit.

PETER AND THE WOLF

S. PROKOFIEFF

PETER'S THEME
Moderato

Copyright © 1960—by ASHLEY PUBLICATIONS

International Copyright Secured.   Made in U.S.A.
All Rights Reserved Including Public Performance for Profit.

THE CAT'S THEME

THE DUCK'S THEME

THE WOLF'S THEME

D.C. al Fine

TO A WATER LILY

EDWARD MAC DOWELL

Copyright © 1960—by ASHLEY PUBLICATIONS

International Copyright Secured.   Made in U.S.A.
All Rights Reserved Including Public Performance for Profit.

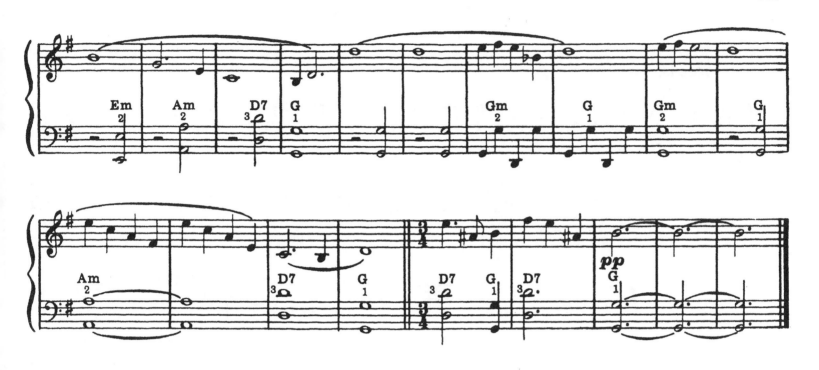

HEARTS AND FLOWERS

T. M. TOBANI

Rather slow

Copyright © 1960—by ASHLEY PUBLICATIONS

International Copyright Secured.   Made in U.S.A.
All Rights Reserved Including Public Performance for Profit.

THE FLATTERER

C. CHAMINADE

Moderato

Copyright © 1960 — by ASHLEY PUBLICATIONS

International Copyright Secured.   Made in U.S.A.
All Rights Reserved Including Public Performance for Profit.

LA CUCARACHA

Allegretto con moto

Copyright © 1960—by ASHLEY PUBLICATIONS

International Copyright Secured.   Made in U.S.A.
All Rights Reserved Including Public Performance for Profit.

LA PALOMA

S. YRADIER

Tempo di Tango

Copyright © 1960—by ASHLEY PUBLICATIONS

International Copyright Secured.   Made in U.S.A.
All Rights Reserved Including Public Performance for Profit.

AY, AY, AY,

Copyright © 1960—by ASHLEY PUBLICATIONS

International Copyright Secured.   Made in U.S.A.
All Rights Reserved Including Public Performance for Profit.

SECOND PIANO CONCERTO

S. RACHMANINOFF

Copyright © 1960—by ASHLEY PUBLICATIONS

International Copyright Secured.   Made in U.S.A.
All Rights Reserved Including Public Performance for Profit.

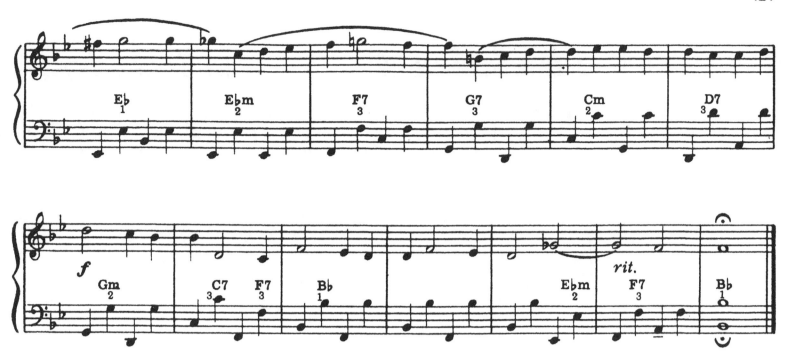

MELODY IN F

A. RUBINSTEIN

Moderately

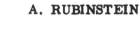

Copyright © 1960 — by ASHLEY PUBLICATIONS

International Copyright Secured.   Made in U.S.A.
All Rights Reserved Including Public Performance for Profit.

CARO NOME

(Rigoletto)

G. VERDI

Moderato

Copyright © 1960—by ASHLEY PUBLICATIONS

International Copyright Secured.   Made in U.S.A.
All Rights Reserved Including Public Performance for Profit.

HEAVENLY AIDA

G. VERDI

Andante

Copyright © 1960—by ASHLEY PUBLICATIONS

International Copyright Secured.   Made in U.S.A.
All Rights Reserved Including Public Performance for Profit.

EL CHOCLO

A. G. VILLOLDO

Copyright © 1960—by ASHLEY PUBLICATIONS

International Copyright Secured.   Made in U.S.A.
All Rights Reserved Including Public Performance for Profit.

D.S. al Fine

NARCISSUS

E. NEVIN

Copyright © 1960—by ASHLEY PUBLICATIONS

International Copyright Secured.   Made in U.S.A.
All Rights Reserved Including Public Performance for Profit.

128

BLUE DANUBE WALTZ

JOHANN STRAUSS

Tempo di Valse

Copyright © 1960—by ASHLEY PUBLICATIONS

International Copyright Secured.   Made in U.S.A.
All Rights Reserved Including Public Performance for Profit.

CLARINET POLKA

Copyright © 1960—by ASHLEY PUBLICATIONS

International Copyright Secured.   Made in U.S.A.
All Rights Reserved Including Public Performance for Profit.

LARGO

G. F. HANDEL

Copyright © 1960—by ASHLEY PUBLICATIONS

International Copyright Secured.   Made in U.S.A.
All Rights Reserved Including Public Performance for Profit.

EVENING STAR

RICHARD WAGNER

Copyright © 1960—by ASHLEY PUBLICATIONS

International Copyright Secured.   Made in U.S.A.
All Rights Reserved Including Public Performance for Profit.

THE STAR SPANGLED BANNER

FRANCIS SCOTT KEY

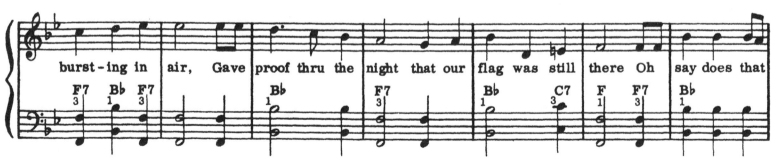

Copyright © 1960—by ASHLEY PUBLICATIONS

International Copyright Secured.   Made in U.S.A.
All Rights Reserved Including Public Performance for Profit.

WHISPERING HOPE

Moderato

A. HAWTHORNE

Copyright © 1960—by ASHLEY PUBLICATIONS

International Copyright Secured.   Made in U.S.A.
All Rights Reserved Including Public Performance for Profit.

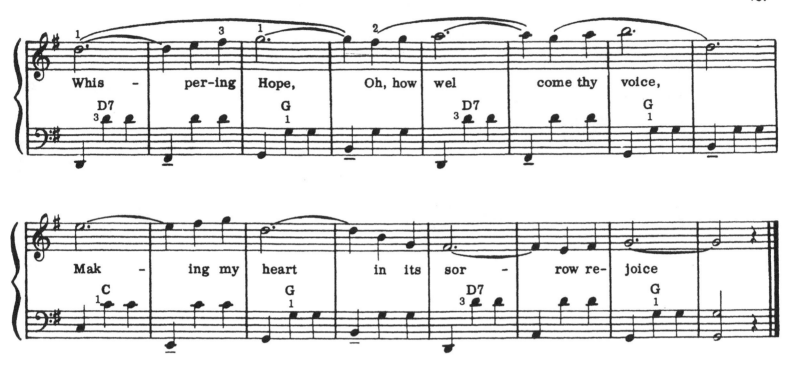

THE LAST ROSE OF SUMMER

Moderato

Copyright © 1960—by ASHLEY PUBLICATIONS

International Copyright Secured.   Made in U.S.A.
All Rights Reserved Including Public Performance for Profit.

COME BACK TO SORRENTO
(Torna A Surriento)

ERNESTO DE CURTIS

Copyright © 1960—by ASHLEY PUBLICATIONS

International Copyright Secured.   Made in U.S.A.
All Rights Reserved Including Public Performance for Profit.

DRINK TO ME ONLY WITH THINE EYES

Moderato

ANDANTE CANTABILE

P. I. TSCHAIKOWSKY

ALOHA OE
(Hawaiian Farewell Song)

QUEEN LYDIA LILIUOKALANI

Andante moderato

THE BAND PLAYED ON

C. B. WARD

Tempo di Valse

CRADLE SONG

JOHANNES BRAHMS

Andante

HOME ON THE RANGE

RED RIVER VALLEY

ADESTE FIDELES
(O Come, All Ye Faithful)

JOHN READING

THE MARINES' HYMN

Tempo di Marcia

BATTLE HYMN OF THE REPUBLIC

T. B. BISHOP

DAISY BELL
(A Bicycle Built For Two)

H. DACRE

I DREAM OF JEANIE

STEPHEN FOSTER

Moderato

HE'S GOT THE WHOLE WORLD IN HIS HANDS

Moderato

He's got the whole world in His hands, He's got the whole world in His hands, He's got the whole world in His hands, He's got the whole world in His hands. He's got the lit-tle ti-ny ba-by in His hands, He's got the lit-tle ti-ny ba-by in His hands, He's got the lit-tle ti-ny ba-by

AULD LANG SYNE

ROBERT BURNS

COCKLES AND MUSCLES

(Molly Malone)

HAND ME DOWN MY WALKING CANE

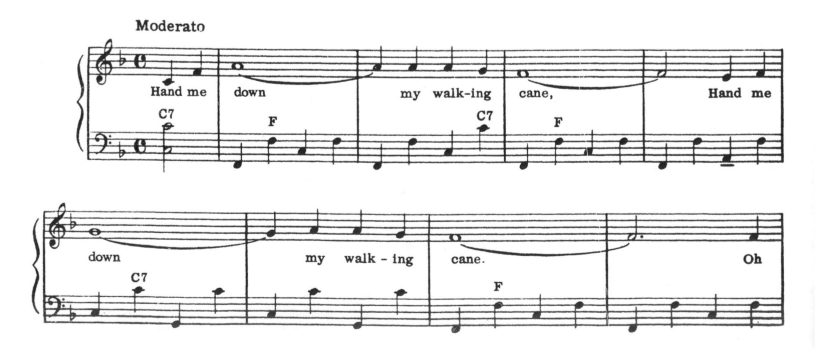

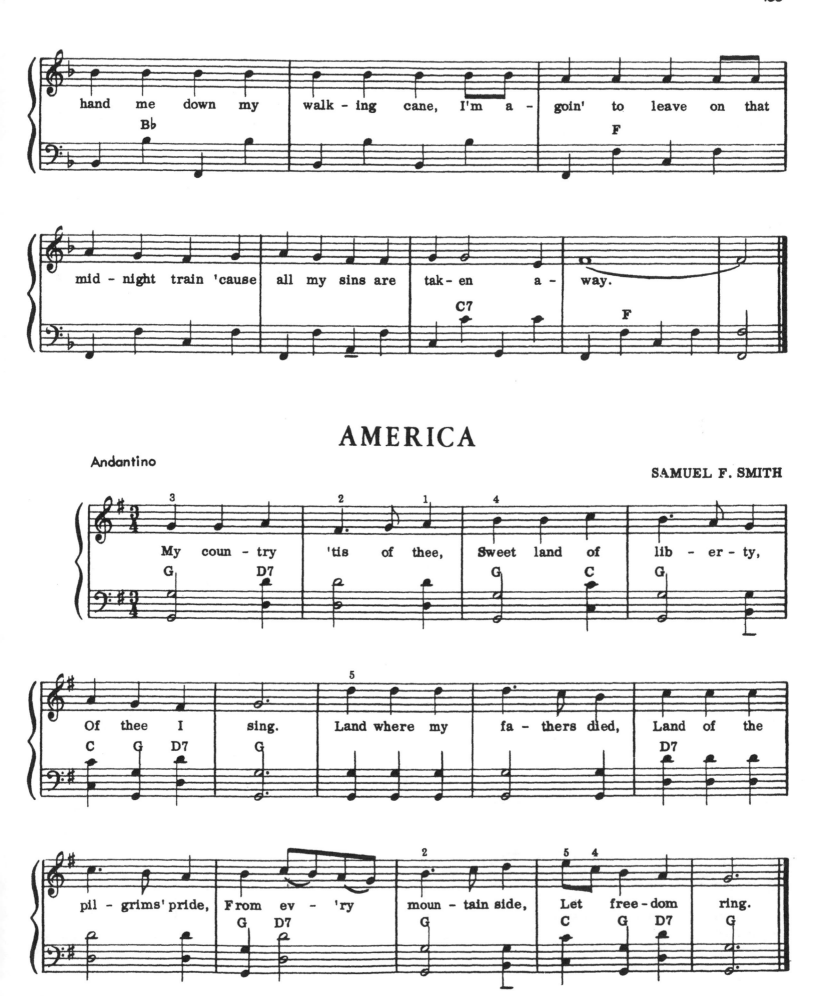

AMERICA

Andantino

SAMUEL F. SMITH

COUNTRY GARDENS

English Dance

Moderato

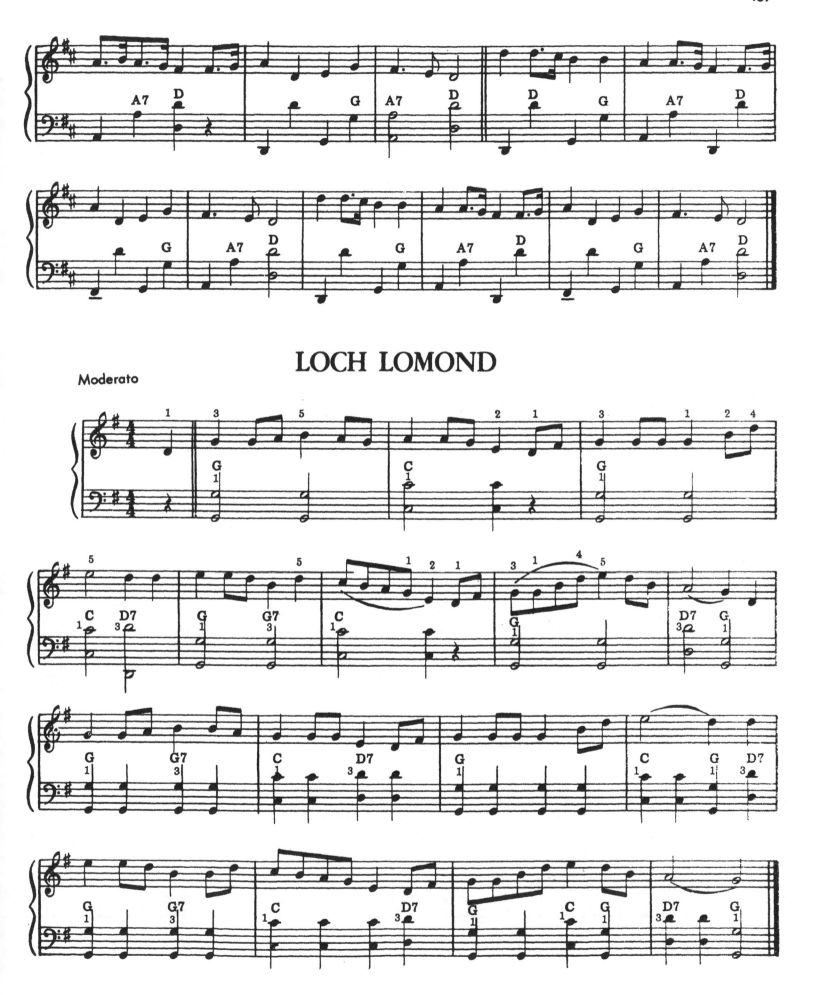

LOCH LOMOND

Moderato

THE YELLOW ROSE OF TEXAS

Moderato

VERSES

1. There's a yel-low rose in Tex-as I'm go-ing there to see No
2. (Where the) Ri-o Grande is flow-ing, where stars are shin-ing bright We
3. (Oh, I'm) go-ing back to find her my heart is full of woe We'll

oth-er fel-low knows her, no-bod-y, on-ly me She
walked a-long the riv-er on a qui-et sum-mer night She
sing the songs to-geth-er we sang so long a-go I'll

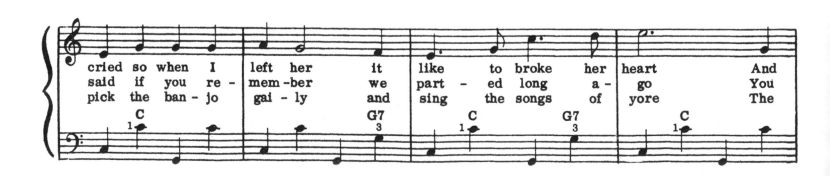

cried so when I left her it like to broke her heart And
said if you re-mem-ber we part-ed long a-go You
pick the ban-jo gai-ly and sing the songs of yore The

Copyright © 1960—by ASHLEY PUBLICATIONS

International Copyright Secured.   Made in U.S.A.
All Rights Reserved Including Public Performance for Profit.

159

VILIA

F. LEHAR

Tempo di Valse

Copyright © 1960—by ASHLEY PUBLICATIONS

International Copyright Secured.   Made in U.S.A.
All Rights Reserved Including Public Performance for Profit.